MAR

W9-AGF-257

Daniel Radcliffe

BY JAN BERNARD

The Child's World

Published by The Child's World®
1980 Lookout Drive • Mankato, MN 56003-1705
800-599-READ • www.childsworld.com

Acknowledgments
The Child's World®: Mary Berendes, Publishing Director
The Design Lab: Cover and interior design
Amnet: Cover and interior production
Red Line Editorial: Editorial direction

Photo credits
Featureflash/Shutterstock Images, cover, 1, 27; Miro Vrlik
Photography LLC/Shutterstock Images, 5; Richard Lewis/
AP Images, 7; Jennifer Graylock/AP Images, 9; Dave Caulkin/
AP Images, 11; Carlos Osorio/AP Images, 13; Peter Mountain/
WireImage/Getty Images, 15; Gareth Davies/Getty Images, 17;
Tammie Arroyo/AP Images, 19; Adam Butler/AP Images, 21;
The Hartman Group, Ari Mintz/AP Images, 23; Joel Ryan/AP
Images, 25; Warner Bros., Jaap Buitendijk/AP Images, 26;
Arthur Mola/AP Images, 29

Design elements
Sergey Shvedov/iStockphoto

ISBN 9781614732907
LCCN 2012933676

Printed in the United States of America
Mankato, Minnesota
July 2012
PA02128

Table of Contents

CHAPTER 1

A Book Comes to Life

"You're a wizard, Harry!" Once Hagrid said these words, life was never the same for Harry Potter. Life was never the same for Daniel Radcliffe either. He was the lucky actor chosen to play Harry in all eight Harry Potter films. The films were based on the popular books by author J. K. Rowling. And the films were huge successes, too. Through November 2011, the movies had made almost $8 billion worldwide.

Few people knew of Daniel before the Harry Potter movies. But Harry is one of the most famous characters ever created. Today millions of people recognize Daniel as Harry Potter. But there is more to Daniel than the Harry Potter character.

Daniel Radcliffe is known around the world for playing Harry Potter.

CHAPTER 2

A Regular Kid in London

Daniel Jacob Radcliffe was born July 23, 1989, in London, England. He is an only child. His dad, Alan, was a **literary agent**. That meant he helped writers get their books published. His mom, Marcia, was a **casting director**. She found just the right person to play roles on television shows, in movies, or in plays.

Daniel's friends knew him simply as Dan. He went to Sussex House. It is a private school for boys in London. He liked his physical education and science classes the best. However, in general, Daniel did not like school very much. He once joked that he would sneak out of class wearing an invisibility cloak. Harry Potter sometimes wore one of those. Whoever wears the magical clothing becomes invisible!

Daniel was never part of the "popular group" at school. He liked kids who were thought to be underdogs instead. They became his best

Daniel was just an ordinary kid before becoming an actor.

friends. He also enjoyed playing *Pokémon* games and watching *The Simpsons* on television.

CHAPTER 3

Acting Is in the Blood

Alan and Marcia had both been actors. Daniel was five when he decided to be an actor, too. He played a monkey in a school play at age six. But his parents did not really want him to make acting his job. They knew how hard it was to get acting jobs. They also knew that fame often causes problems for young actors. But Daniel did not give up. His parents finally gave in. They let him act in a 1999 television movie called *David Copperfield*. He also acted in the 2001 film *The Tailor of Panama*. Daniel's parents still did not want their son starting an acting career, though. After all, he was only ten years old.

Daniel had smaller acting roles before he became Harry Potter.

CHAPTER 4

Who Will Play Harry?

Many people had read a Harry Potter book by 2001. Each reader got to decide what he or she thought Harry looked like. One actress on *The Tailor of Panama* had an idea. She thought Harry Potter looked just like Daniel! There must have been magic in the air. Exciting things soon started happening for the young actor.

The first Harry Potter film was *Harry Potter and the Sorcerer's Stone*. More than 10,000 boys tried out for the role of Harry Potter. But director Chris Columbus was not happy with any of them. Time was running out for him to make a choice. Filming was set to begin in two months. Columbus still had not selected an actor to play Harry Potter.

Daniel jokes with *Harry Potter and the Sorcerer's Stone* director Chris Columbus.

Columbus had a video of a child he thought would be perfect. But the child's parents did not want him to **audition**. The video Columbus had was *David Copperfield*. And the kid he was looking at was Daniel.

CHAPTER 5

A Wizard Is Born

Sometimes things happen in magical ways. Daniel went to see a play one night in London. It was hard for Daniel to pay attention, though. That is because two men kept turning around to look at him. Daniel did not know who they were. It turned out the men were a **producer** and a **screenwriter**. They were working on *Harry Potter and the Sorcerer's Stone*.

They thought Daniel looked like Harry, too. The producer knew Daniel's father. He talked Alan and Marcia into letting Daniel try out. Daniel's parents were still nervous, though. The books were already

Daniel's likeness was made into an action figure for the first Harry Potter movie.

very popular. That meant the actor who played Harry would likely become an instant star. Alan and Marcia worried that the part might bring too much **publicity** to Daniel. That could put a lot of pressure on the boy. The producer and screenwriter understood the parents' concerns. So they promised to work with the family to protect Daniel.

Daniel still had to go through auditions. But from the start everyone knew he would play Harry. Daniel was in the bathtub when he got the call. He would officially be playing Harry Potter! Daniel was so excited that he cried. The excitement even prevented

Harry Potter series author J. K. Rowling knew right away that Daniel was a perfect fit. She said it felt like she had reunited with a long-lost son. Daniel had passed the last hurdle to becoming Harry Potter.

Daniel acts in *Harry Potter and the Sorcerer's Stone.*

him from sleeping. Daniel woke his parents up
at two in the morning to make sure it was not all
a dream.

CHAPTER 6

The Magic Begins

Daniel stayed pretty calm until the first day of shooting. Harry Potter has a famous scar on his forehead. That scar had to be put on Daniel's head using makeup. That is when everything began to feel real. He told CNN that he hoped he did not mess everything up!

Daniel was a pretty serious kid. He loved to play pranks, though. There were many opportunities for that on the set. One of Daniel's favorite pranks involved setting people's cell phones to different languages. Scottish actor Robbie Coltrane played the character Hagrid in the movies. One time, Daniel set Coltrane's phone to Turkish.

Daniel was one of three child costars in the Harry Potter films. Emma Watson played Hermione

Daniel smiles with Harry Potter series author J. K. Rowling in 2001.

Granger. Rupert Grint played Ron Weasley. The three actors quickly became best friends. They found that their own personalities were a lot like the characters they played.

Daniel's life began changing as soon as the first movie came out. Suddenly, he was a global star. Fame sometimes leads some actors to change. Famous actors get many new opportunities. Sometimes they get new friends. Daniel said his friends and his parents helped keep the fame from going to his head.

Daniel once said the hardest part of being famous was signing autographs. That was because his name is so long!

Harry Potter actors *(from left)* Rupert Grint, Daniel, and Emma Watson became big stars.

CHAPTER 7

Everybody Loves Harry

Daniel originally signed on to act in two Harry Potter films. The director had planned to replace the three main characters after the third film. However, he later changed his mind. Instead, it became a race to finish all eight films before the actors got too old.

Daniel has received a lot of praise for his acting in the Harry Potter films. In 2007, he joined Emma and Rupert in Hollywood, California. They left their marks. Many celebrities leave their handprints in the sidewalk in front of Grauman's Chinese Theater. The Harry Potter stars left prints of their hands, feet, and wands!

Daniel (*right*) and his Harry Potter costars acted in all eight movies in the series.

Playing such a famous character has many benefits. However, it can also have drawbacks. Some people wondered if Daniel would be able to have any other acting roles. After all, everybody would look at him as Harry Potter. But Daniel made an effort to branch out. He took other acting roles between Harry Potter films. In 2007, he was in a play called *Equus*. He sang, danced, and acted in another play in 2011. It was called *How to Succeed in Business Without Really Trying*.

The final Harry Potter film came out in 2011. In 2012 Daniel starred in the film *The Woman in Black*. It was about a ghost.

Daniel has always enjoyed music. So actor Gary Oldman (Sirius Black) gave Daniel a bass guitar as a gift the first time they met. He gave Daniel lessons, too!

Daniel performs in *How to Succeed in Business Without Really Trying.*

CHAPTER 8

A Magical Life

In most ways, Daniel is just like everyone else. He even gets starstruck when he meets other famous actors. Daniel had more freedom once he became an adult. He could have lived wherever he wanted. After all, he was one of the richest people in England. But he still chose to live near his parents' home. He knew his friends and parents would keep him out of trouble.

Life has not always been easy for Daniel, though. Like many people, he has a learning disability. It is called **dyspraxia**. Daniel has a mild form of the disability. So he did not have trouble reading or memorizing his lines as a child. But simple things

Harry Potter fans watched as *(from left)* **Daniel, Emma, and Rupert grew into young adults on screen.**

could be hard for him. He had trouble tying his shoes and writing. Part of the reason Daniel disliked school was that he felt like he was bad at anything he tried. That was because of the dyspraxia. However, many kids with dyspraxia learn how to be more

Daniel leads his costars in *Harry Potter and the Deathly Hallows Part 2.*

Fans were excited to see Daniel before the final Harry Potter movie was released in London, England.

coordinated as they grow older. That has happened for Daniel, too.

Daniel did not let the dyspraxia stand in his way. He loves to write short stories and poems. In fact, he published a book of poems under the pen name Jacob Gershon. He took Jacob from his middle name. Gershon was the Jewish version of his mom's maiden name.

Many fans watched Daniel grow up as Harry Potter on the big screen. The movie series is now complete, but Daniel's acting career is only just getting started. The next play or movie you see might just be starring everyone's favorite wizard!

Daniel is a big cricket fan. Cricket is a sport similar to baseball that is popular in England and other countries.

The future is bright for Daniel.

GLOSSARY

audition (aw-DISH-uhn): An audition is when actors try out for a role in plays or films. The film studio held an audition to find an actor to play Harry Potter.

casting director (CAST-ing duh-REK-tur): A casting director finds actors to play roles in plays, on television, and in movies. Daniel's mom was a casting director.

dyspraxia (dis-PRAX-see-uh): Dyspraxia is a disability that involves difficulty with movement. Daniel suffers from a mild form of dyspraxia.

literary agent (LIT-ur-air-ee AY-juhnt): A literary agent arranges the sale of books or scripts to publishers. Daniel's dad was a literary agent.

producer (pruh-DOOS-ur): A producer finds the money to make a movie and supervises the making and distribution of the movie. A producer for the Harry Potter films first discovered Daniel.

publicity (puh-BLIS-i-tee): Publicity is interest or attention. Daniel received much publicity for playing Harry Potter.

screenwriter (SKREEN RITE-ur): A screenwriter writes scripts for movies, television shows, or plays. A screenwriter wrote the script for the Harry Potter films.

FURTHER INFORMATION

BOOKS

Norwich, Grace. *Daniel Radcliffe: No Ordinary Wizard.* New York: Simon Spotlight, 2008.

Rawson, Katherine. *Daniel Radcliffe.* New York: PowerKids Press, 2010.

Rowling, J. K. *Harry Potter and the Sorcerer's Stone.* New York: Scholastic, 1999.

WEB SITES

Visit our Web site for links about Daniel Radcliffe: **childsworld.com/links**

Note to Parents, Teachers, and Librarians: We routinely verify our Web links to make sure they are safe and active sites. So encourage your readers to check them out!

INDEX

ABOUT THE AUTHOR

Jan Bernard has been an elementary teacher in both Ohio and in Georgia, and has written curriculum for schools for over seven years. She also is the author of seven books. She lives in West Jefferson, Ohio, with her husband and their dog, Nigel. She has two sons.